12 Myths That Could Wreck Your Golf Game

Excerpts from The Search for the Perfect Golf Club

Tom Wishon
with Tom Grundner

SMG
SPORTS
MEDIA
GROUP

All inquiries should be addressed to:
Sports Media Group
An imprint of Ann Arbor Media Group LLC
2500 S. State Street
Ann Arbor, MI 48104

ISBN 13: 978-1-58726-316-3
ISBN 10: 1-58726-316-5

CONTENTS

Introduction

The game of golf is treading water these days.

Each year about the same number of people leave the game as start playing. When surveyed, one of the major reasons given by those who give up golf is "frustration with the game."

This fact led noted golf club designer Tom Wishon to ask: how much of that frustration is the result of a game that is, admittedly, inherently frustrating to even the best players; and how much of it is caused by "equipment-induced frustration"? How many of those golfers simply hit a "grass ceiling" where they found themselves trapped in a nightmare of publicly embarrassing poor performance caused by equipment that not only would not—but *could not possibly*—meet their needs. Thinking they are playing with equipment that is properly designed and fitted (after all, they paid enough for the stuff), they can then only ascribe their failings to themselves—to their own ineptitude—and give up on the game.

To help deal with this problem, in 2005 Wishon wrote *The Search for the Perfect Golf Club,* which became an immediate success. It was the first book to explain to the average golfer, in simple terms, how golf clubs worked, how you can make them perform better for YOUR game, what to look for (and look out for) in buying clubs, and much more. Chief among his assertions is that *all golfers—from beginners to single-digit handicappers—will directly and immediately benefit from custom built clubs,* and that perfecting this area will be the next major frontier in golf.

The Search for the Perfect Golf Club has become the one book that every golfer needs to own and read! Excerpts in *12 Myths* will introduce you to Wishon's work in an entertaining way.

After reading this mini-book, we're sure you will agree that the full version of *The Search for the Perfect Golf Club* belongs in YOUR library.

Myth 1

Modern golf clubs hit farther than clubs of
even a few years ago.

In reality, no, they don't. What you are seeing basically is a marketing gimmick.

Let's begin at the beginning.

Three things primarily determine the distance you hit a golf ball: the loft of the clubhead, the length of the shaft, and the speed with which you swing. There is also a time proven adage about golf clubs—the longer the length, the lower the loft, the heavier the weight, and the stiffer the shaft, the harder the club will be to hit. Over the past few years your body's swing speed has probably stayed about the same, but the loft angles and the shaft length of your clubs have not.

Each year, in order to say their clubs "hit farther," the club companies have been tinkering with the loft angles on the faces of your clubheads—lowering them a bit at a time each year. As a result, every club in the set has moved "up" at least one, if not two, numbers. So, when you go to a driving range for "demo day" and you are hitting a 6-iron farther than you hit your old 5-iron, you now know why. It's because that shiny new 6-iron in your hands *was* a 5-iron only a few years ago and probably a 4-iron a few years before that.

In some ways these changes would be comical if they didn't have such sad results. Now golfers carry clubs that are, in effect, designed from the factory to be unhittable in the hands of the average golfer and are forced to buy additional clubs that they otherwise would not have needed.

Again, let me start with some background.

In the world of club design there is something called the "24/38 Rule." Basically, it says that the average golfer cannot hit an iron that has less than 24 degrees of loft or more than 38 inches of length. The reason is that a club like that requires a swing precision that the average golfer rarely has the opportunity to attain.

Table 1—The Dreaded Vanishing Loft Disease

Evolution of Men's Wood & Iron Lofts—Industry Average

Club	1960s–70s (degrees)	1980s (degrees)	Early 1990s (degrees)	1997+ (degrees)
1-iron	17	17	16	16–17
2-iron	20	20	19	18–20
3-iron	24	23	22	20–21
4-iron	28	26	25	23–24
5-iron	32	30	28	26–27
6-iron	36	34	32	30–31
7-iron	40	38	36	34–35
8-iron	44	42	40	38–40
9-iron	48	46	44	42–44
PW	52	50	48	46–48
SW	56	56	56	55–56
Driver	11	11	10	9–10.5
3-wood	16	15	15	13–14
5-wood	22	21	19	17–18
7-wood	28	27	23	20–21

Note: A quick look at the information above shows how drastically golf club companies have reduced their loft angles over the past few decades. This was done primarily so they could say their clubs hit the ball farther and thereby sell more clubs.

A few years ago the 24/38 line fell on the other side of the 3-iron. So, when you bought a set of clubs, you bought a 3-iron through pitching wedge and you could reasonably expect to hit each of those clubs. Because of the "vanishing loft disease" I just described, the 24/38 line has now moved to just the shy side of the 5-iron—making the 3- and 4-iron unhittable for most people.

So, what are you supposed to do? It's simple. The club companies want you *to buy three more clubs* to compensate for the corner that *they* painted you into. You are now supposed to buy something called "hybrid" clubs, which are easy-to-hit substitutes for the 3- and 4-irons that are no longer hittable by the majority of golfers. In addition, as all the irons have now moved up and away from the sand wedge, you are now supposed to buy something called a "gap wedge" to fill in the "gap" *they* created with their loft-shrinking marketing stunts.

For more information on this topic refer to *The Search for the Perfect Golf Club*: "The Dreaded Vanishing Loft Disease" (pg. 7) and "Set Makeup and the 24/38 Rule" (pg. 139).

Myth 2

The longer my driver is, the farther I'll be able to hit the ball.

In my estimation, 90 percent of the drivers sold in the shops today are too long for most players. If that's the case for you, then get it cut down and re-swing-weighted to the shorter length, and don't be shy about doing it. Here's why:

Let's start with the issue of distance. Most golfers believe that longer length drivers will hit farther. They won't. Drivers ranging from 43 to 45 inches were put to a test with 50 different golfers of varying handicap levels. Here are the data. Read it for yourself. The difference in distance between a 43- and a 45-inch driver is a whopping yard plus inches. Accuracy wise, there is no question that the old adage of "the longer the length, the harder the club is to hit" certainly rings true.

But wait. The plot thickens.

There is another reason for having a shorter driver. It appears that, in the hands of real people the shorter driver might very well hit the ball, not just with more accuracy but more distance as well.

For every quarter inch you miss the sweet spot on your driver, you lose about five yards in distance. Miss it by a half inch and you lose 10 yards; an inch, 20 yards, and so forth.

Conversely, if you can gain enough control of the club to hit the ball even a half inch closer to the sweet spot, you'll not only enjoy the distance increase that comes with a more solid impact but you'll be more likely to keep the ball on the fairway.

Okay, fine. So most golfers today are using clubs that are too long to allow

Golfer Handicap Group	Driver Length (inches)	Average Distance (carry in yards)	Average Misdirection (yards off center of fairway)
24 to 36	45	206.4	+/− 25.3
	44	207.0	+/− 21.3
	43	207.3	+/− 16.7
18 to 23	45	214.2	+/− 26.4
	44	214.8	+/− 22.7
	43	215.7	+/− 17.0
12 to 17	45	221.3	+/− 23.5
	44	222.5	+/− 18.1
	43	222.8	+/− 15.1
6 to 11	45	227.1	+/− 18.2
	44	228.1	+/− 15.6
	43	228.4	+/− 11.8
0 to 5	45	238.7	+/− 15.7
	44	238.3	+/− 12.2
	43	237.5	+/− 9.7

them to play their best. How do you know what the right length is for you? Most people assume that if they are taller than 6'2" or shorter than 5'8", they might need "inch-over" or "inch-under" length clubs. Nothing could be farther from the truth.

The length of your clubs is not determined by your height; it is determined by the length of your arms, and then massaged from there to the final length by your swing plane and ball striking ability! A custom clubmaker works with one basic principle in mind:

> The proper length for all golfers is the longest length that the golfer can hit SOLID AND ON-CENTER the highest percentage of the time. Truth is, when it comes to your woods that length is undoubtedly shorter than what you are using now.

The way a clubmaker determines proper length is by first measuring the distance from the golfer's wrist to the floor and referencing that dimension to a chart developed over years of fitting research to guide the initial club length recommendations. Fitting length is not done through a fingertip to floor measurement, but wrist to floor. The reason is because of the wide variance people have in finger length and the fact that the end of your grip lines up closer to where your wrists are in the grip. The wrist measurement is a more reliable measurement to indicate arm length. The size of your hands or length of your fingers is only relevant to grip fitting and not club length.

Table 2—Wrist-to-Floor Measurement for Initial Club Lengths (inches)

Wrist-to-Floor	Driver Length	5-Iron Length
27 to 29	42	36.5
29 to 32	42.5	37
32 to 34	43	37.5
34 to 36	43.5	38
36 to 37	44	38.25
37 to 38	44.25	38.5
38 to 39	44.5	38.75
39 to 40	44.75	39
40 to 41	45	39.25
41 to 42	45.5	39.5
over 42	46 and up	39.75 and up

Note: A wrist-to floor measurement is used as the initial guideline for determining club lengths for the golfer that will match well with their height and arm length for comfort. To make the measurement correctly, wear flat-sole shoes only, stand comfortably erect, shoulders perfectly level, arms hanging relaxed at the sides. The measurement is made from the major wrist crease on the dominant hand to the floor in inches plus any fraction.

So, proper length fitting starts with a length recommendation based on the golfer's wrist-to-floor measurement. But, that is just the beginning. After the initial length from the wrist-to-floor measurement is determined, a good custom fitter will look at both your swing plane and your swing tempo as well as your ability to athletically control the club during the swing. Only after those data are factored in will a final length recommendation be made.

For more information on this topic, refer to *The Search for the Perfect Golf Club*: "A-R-G-G-H!! Drivers" (pg. 150) and "Finding the Right Length" (pg. 146).

Myth 3

The lower the loft on my driver, the farther I
will hit the ball.

Yup, this statement is true ... if your name happens to be John Daly. For the rest of us mere mortals, to get more distance off the tee you will probably need a HIGHER loft. I know that sounds counter-intuitive so let me explain it this way.

I am sure at one time or another you've played around with a garden hose. Imagine you have the hose turned on full blast and you are trying to get as much distance as possible out of the water spray. Now, suppose someone turns the water pressure back by about a third. You can feel the drop in pressure in your hands and see it in the loss of distance in the spray. So, what do you automatically do to try to get that distance back? Exactly! You raise the angle of the nozzle.

It's the same thing with the driver.

If you have a very fast swing speed (i.e., the hose is on full blast), you need a lower loft to get maximum distance. If you have a slower swing speed (i.e., the hose pressure has been cut back), you need a *higher* loft to get more distance. *What you CANNOT do is match a slow swing speed with a low-lofted driver.* That is the equivalent of lowering the water pressure *and* lowering the nozzle angle, and wondering why the water isn't going as far.

If you still doubt me, look at the numbers in table 3. Look at the listing for a 90 mph swing speed (based on a +2.5 degree upward angle of attack in the swing, which is about average for most men with a driver. The distance achieved by your "water hose" increases as the launch angle (loft) goes UP, not down. This holds until you get to about 13 degrees of loft, when the distance goes down again. If the angle of attack from your swing is level or downward, you'll need even more loft to achieve your maximum carry distance. (Don't have a clue about your angle of attack? Don't worry. *The Search for the Perfect Golf Club* teaches you how to determine it.)

Table 3—The Effect of Launch Angle on Driver Distance[a]

Swing Speed (mph)	Driver Loft (degrees)	Launch Angle (degrees)	Carry Distance (yards)
60	11	12.1	106
	15	15.2	117
	19	18.1	122
70	11	12.1	145
	15	15.2	154
	19	18.1	156
80	9	10.5	174
	11	12.1	181
	13	13.7	185
90	9	10.5	206
	11	12.1	211
	13	13.7	213
100	8	9.6	231
	9	10.5	234
	10	12.1	236
110	7	8.8	254
	8	9.6	256
	9	10.5	257

Note: To achieve maximum distance, every golfer from pro to beginner must be fitted with the correct driver loft angle to match their swing speed. It is the only way to obtain the best launch angle for maximum distance.

[a]Table information is based on a swing angle of attack of +2.5 degrees, which means hitting the ball on the upswing with the driver traveling upward at an angle of 2.5 degrees. The average golfer will have a slight upward angle of attack with the driver. For golfers who do not hit the ball on the upswing, the optimum driver loft for maximum distance will be a little higher loft than what is shown in the table.

So, how fast can you reasonably expect to swing your driver WITH CONTROL? The only way to know for sure is to be measured by a professional golf clubmaker; but here are some numbers that might give you a sense of where you probably are.

Average Female Golfer: 65 mph

Average Male Golfer: 85 mph

Average Female Tour Player: 97 mph

Average Male Tour Player: 110 mph

Male Long Drive Competitors: 135–155 mph

You still want that 9- or 10-degree driver? To get the maximum distance out of a 10-degree driver, you need a swing speed (with control!) of about 100 mph. To get maximum distance out of a 9-degree driver, swing speed needs to be about 110 mph. The rest of us (in the 80 and 90-something mph speed ranges) will get maximum distance from 11-, 12-, and 13-degree clubs. For most women and slower swinging senior men, it's going to take a 14-degree or higher loft on the driver to maximize your distance.

> For more information on this topic, refer to *The Search for the Perfect Golf Club:* "Backspin, Loft, and Distance" (pg. 13).

Myth 4

The bigger the head, the better

You know, sometimes it must seem like the golf companies have a big air pump in their factories that they use to make last year's driver even larger in order to announce the "new and improved" model is now here. I mean, even the USGA became so concerned about it that they finally said: Enough, we'll let you stay with heads the size of grapefruit, but no way are we going to let you go to watermelons. Now, if you believe that the USGA imposes restrictions on equipment to keep designers from making the game too easy, then you would probably conclude that bigger must be better, right?

No, that's not quite true, at least not for the reason you are probably thinking.

You see, theoretically, it's possible to design a bigger driver head, with a bigger face area that has a greater "spring-face" effect, thus increasing the ball speed off the face and giving you more distance. But remember the big battle a few years ago over the amount of "spring" (known as the coefficient of restitution) that was allowable on the clubface? At that point, the USGA put the handcuffs on the maximum allowable spring in a driver face, and any possibility of increasing driver head size to make the face "spring more" was eliminated.

So when we designers make bigger and bigger drivers, we also have to make the faces thicker and thicker to prevent them from generating a ball speed that would exceed the USGA's rule for spring-face effect. And that, gentle reader, cancels out any possible advantage of bigger heads being better.

So what's left? How can we make a bigger head be a better head? There IS one way, but it's only for a certain segment of players who need it.

In general, the bigger the head the farther back the center of gravity (CG) will be. That will bring about an increase in the height of the shot over a smaller head of the same loft, when using the same shaft. So, if you need a higher ball flight to improve your carry distance, you could just go with an oversized head whose center of gravity has been moved aft. The problem is that you're taking a risk that when the manufacturer says the club has a "more rear-located CG," that it really HAS a "more rear-located CG." It's much more of a sure thing to optimize your launch angle for your swing speed via the club's loft.

One last point. Can we get it out of our heads that because your clubhead is made of titanium (or similar hard material) that it will hit the ball farther?

At one point or another, drivers have been made from nearly everything—wood, steel, plastic, aluminum, graphite, titanium, and even ceramics. Along the way, the marketing geeks decided they had free reign to tout almost any non-wooden object as the "next greatest" golf club. If the material was harder than wood, it had to hit the ball farther, right? Well, the answer is "no," but that doesn't slow down the marketers a bit.

The vast majority of drivers today are made from some variety of titanium because titanium possesses "the right stuff." More specifically, it has the right combination of lightness and strength and elasticity so that your oversized clubhead will not collapse like a cheap tent the first time you smash into a golf ball.

Clubhead hardness has *nothing* to do with how far the ball will travel. It might affect how easily your club gets banged up in the bag, but distance? No way. And there are all sorts of research studies to prove it.

As far as the hardness and strength (or lack thereof) affecting your ability to work the ball flight, again, there is no way. Workability (the ability to intentionally fade or draw the ball) is all about the club's *design*. How is the weight distributed? Where is the center of gravity? What is its moment of inertia? These have nothing to do with the type of metal being used.

That's why, when you buy clubs, you need to consult with someone like your local professional clubmaker who knows which metallurgical advances are for real (and why) and which are gimmicks.

For more information on this topic, refer to *The Search for the Perfect Golf Club:* "Big, Bigger, and Biggest" (pg. 59) and "The Right Stuff" (pg. 40).

Myth 5

I know I play a stiff shaft; it says so right on it.

No, you don't know that you are playing a stiff shaft. The "S" you see on your shaft is completely meaningless.

Most golfers know, or think they know, that shafts come in a variety of flexes: S for stiff, R for regular, A for amateur or senior, and L for ladies. What most golfers don't realize is that those letters (and only those letters) represent just about everything upon which there is universal agreement.

You say you want a "stiff" shaft in your driver? Fine. Whose definition of *stiff* do you want to use? Because one shaft company's "stiff," is another company's "regular," which is another company's "A-flex." Worse, the flex rating of one line of shafts might be at hopeless variance with that of another line, within the same shaft company!

But, I'm just getting started.

Is that "stiff" shaft going into an iron or a wood? Because iron "stiffs" are stiffer than wood "stiffs." And you've said nothing about whether you want that driver in a steel shaft whose "stiff" is almost always stiffer than a graphite shaft.

If it sounds as if the concept of shaft flex is hosed to the point of being a shot in the dark for your game, you are exactly right. If you buy a driver because it has a stiff, regular, senior, or ladies flex shaft in it, you have *no idea* what you are getting—nor does anyone else.

Wait a minute; let me retract that. Serious, professional clubmakers do. They have easy access to that kind of information; golf stores do not.

Here's the bottom line.

> From a pure shaft performance standpoint, 90 percent of you are going to be better off with a shaft that is more flexible than what you think you need.

Let me put it this way. If you happen to end up with a shaft that is too stiff for your swing speed and your swing mechanics, first, the ball will go a little shorter in distance because it will probably fly a little lower. Second, you might have a tendency to see the ball fly over to the fade side of the target. Your feeling from hitting the ball on the center of the face will be a little more "harsh," as if the club felt like it vibrated a little more in the hands.

On the other hand, if you happened to end up with a shaft that is too flexible for your swing, first, the ball might fly a little higher and from that, possibly, a little farther. Second, it might cause a fade shot to fade a little less or a draw shot to draw a little more. The feeling of an on-center impact on the clubface will bring a softer or more solid feeling to your hands. Of the two, choosing the second choice is a no brainer.

> Unless you work with a professional clubmaker to make your shaft selection, you will have to do a lot of trial-and-error test hitting of all sorts of shafts before you come up with a decision.

You might be able to guess that you want to have an R- or an S-flex, for example, but because the R from one company can be very different in stiffness from the R of another, you have no other alternatives but to: (a) do trial-and-error testing to see for yourself how stiff or flexible that new R- or S-flex shaft really is compared to your old one; or (b) listen to a retail sales person who nine times out of ten won't know enough about shafts to really help ensure you get the right one for your swing.

You might be measured for your swing speed in a retail golf store, but I am here to tell you that virtually NONE of the big companies that make the standard golf clubs stocked in the retail shops ever provide their retailers with a reference chart to indicate what swing speed matches up with which flex in each shaft model they offer. So, the recommendation of the retail sales person will quite possibly be a guess or based on which flex they have more of in their store inventory.

A competent clubmaker will measure your swing speed, and then observe your swing mechanics to look for things like your tempo, how much force you use to start the downswing, and where in the downswing you release your wrist-cock. The clubmaker will then ask you some questions about how high or low you want to see the ball fly and other performance-goal queries to determine what you want to achieve that could be associated with the shaft's performance. He or she will then reference the files of shaft information that he gets from his suppliers or from research on shaft testing that they or other clubmakers have done and made available to each other. He will also have more precise lists of what swing speed matches well to what shaft flex for what shaft design. After that, he will make a recommendation and possibly build a test club for you to hit to obtain feedback. The clubmaker may also have a launch monitor which can be used to actually measure the launch angle contribution of the shaft as you swing the club. And in the end, the clubmaker will come up with a far more accurate recommendation of which shaft is likely to perform and feel best to YOU.

> For more information on this topic, refer to *The Search for the Perfect Golf Club:* "A Term with a Lot of Flex in It" (pg. 97).

Myth 6

The newer clubs have a larger "sweet spot."

Actually, they don't. What they might have, however, is a larger "moment of inertia" and that is a very different thing.

Sweet spot is a term that is commonly found in golf club ads and misused a lot by almost everyone in the golf industry. You frequently see ads boasting that this club or that has a "larger" or "wider" sweet spot. Technically that can't happen because the actual sweet spot (officially known as the center of gravity) is a point that's about the size of the sharp end of a pin. It can't get "larger." It can't get "smaller." It just…is.

If you deliver the face of the club square to impact and hit the exact center of the golf ball directly in line with this tiny spot, the ball will fly straight, true, and at the highest speed your swing will allow. But, here's the catch. If you miss this point of perfect contact, the head will start to twist, not only imparting sidespin to the ball but causing a loss of distance. As mentioned earlier, if you miss the sweet spot by a quarter inch, you lose five yards, a half inch, 10 yards, and so forth.

The only way to help relieve this problem is by making heads that resist twisting as much as possible. In technical terms, that's called increasing their "moment of inertia." But don't panic over these terms. You know all about moment of inertia because you've seen it in action dozens of times.

Think of a figure skater doing a spin. When their arms are out, their moment of inertia (i.e., their resistance to twisting) is increased, so they spin more slowly. When they draw their arms in close to their body, their moment of inertia is immediately decreased, so they spin faster. Hence, low moment of inertia (MOI), less resistance to twisting—high MOI (a neat buzzword acronym you can use on your golf buddies) more resistance to twisting (see fig. 1).

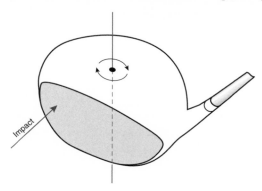

Figure 1. The amount the head twists around an axis straight through the center of gravity in response to an off-center hit is determined by the clubhead's Moment of Inertia. The higher the MOI of the head, the less the head twists and the higher the ball speed will be from the off-center hit. Moving more of the head's weight around the perimeter of the head increases the clubhead's MOI.

Well, the same thing happens with the golf clubhead. The clubhead has some natural resistance to twisting around its center of gravity (moment of inertia), which can be increased, for example, by putting extra weight out at the heel and toe and back of the clubhead (i.e., by extending the club head's "arms"). The more you can do that, the more resistance to twisting you have, the "larger" (i.e., more forgiving) is the so-called sweet spot. That's really what they are talking about when they say the "sweet spot is larger."

One final point. The moment of inertia of a clubhead is especially important with putters. Basically, the higher the MOI, the better the putter will perform when you look up or move or do whatever you do to hit the ball somewhere other than the sweet spot. So, when you are thinking about buying a putter, look at the heel and toe and rear areas. If you see gobs of weight in those areas, compared to the front or the middle, you know you are on the right track. In addition, putters that are much longer from face to back will also provide a better chance of reaching the hole with any putt you hit off the sweet spot.

But you will never, ever, putt well with any putter no matter how elevated its MOI unless you are fitted properly for the correct lie, length, loft, grip feel, and overall weight or balance of the putter.

For more information on this topic, refer to *The Search for the Perfect Golf Club*: "Home Sweet Spot" (pg. 36).

Myth 7

Women's clubs are designed for women.

It pains me to say this, but, by and large, the women get a raw deal when it comes to golf equipment. Male golfers get to choose from several different head designs, driver lofts, and shaft flexes, in steel or graphite. Women get to choose from one head model, maybe two but usually only one driver loft, and one flex of one model of shaft in one length.

If you applied the golf industry's approach to equipment selection for women to the clothing industry, here's what you would see in your local department store. You would walk through the men's department and see the usual array of sizes and styles from small to XXX-large, but when you get to the women's department, you would see clothing offered in only two or three styles and only in size small.

The same thing is true in the "senior golfer" department. The customer would only see limited styles and "one size" from which to meet their clothing needs. With regard to women...have you ever seen a golf club marketed to "senior women"? Right. Like senior women don't play golf?

In the average retail golf store, the regular men's clubs account for close to 90 percent of all the clubs in the store. Lofts on drivers are stocked from 8 to 12 degrees and flexes on both graphite and steel shafts in R, S, and X. For women's clubs, however, drivers are usually stocked in a 12- or 13-degree loft, lengths are an inch shorter than the corresponding men's model; and shafts are offered in only one flex.

The problem is that the vast majority of "average" female golfers need drivers with more loft than what is offered, shorter lengths for all the woods, a set makeup that eliminates the 3- and 4-iron (and probably even the 5-iron thanks to the "vanishing loft" disease of modern irons) completely from consideration, and a choice of at least two different shaft flexes that should be more flexible than any men's shaft.

But it gets worse.

Most people assume that a women's golf clubhead is based on the men's, but represents a fresh design and a unique casting. Sometimes that is true, but it is unusual. If you were to compare the specifications of, let's say, a random set of women's irons and a set of men's, you might be surprised to find that the loft, lie, weight, and design features are exactly the same. They are simply men's clubs that are marketed to women.

Then we have the shafts themselves. Earlier we discussed the problem of shaft flex at some length. We pointed out that shaft flex is not standardized and, therefore, its letter code designations for flex are virtually meaningless.

Regarding women's shafts, we have to amend that conclusion. With the L-flexes, the results of the study were both predictable and meaningful. Every one of the shafts they tested was out of sequence compared to the other A, R, S, and X shaft flexes. They were ALL too stiff for a female golfer with a 65 mph swing speed—especially when cut and installed to the final assembly length.

Terrific.

To be fair, a few shaft companies have recently come out with what they call an "LL-Flex." Translated, the LL-flex means: "We-finally-figured-out-there-are-differences-in-female-golfers'-swing-speeds-just-like-there-are-with-men-so-we-decided-to-finally-do-what-we-do-for-men-and-offer-you-a-choice." I look forward to seeing the data that confirm the LL-flex as being what it is supposed to be. If it is, it'll be a breakthrough.

The point here is that there are women, senior, and even some junior golfers who can and should play with the same fitting specifications that you would find in men's clubs. And there are some men who can and should be playing with what are labeled by the golf industry as "senior" or "lady" club specifications. The only way to know is to be properly and professionally fitted.

Just because someone put pink, taupe, or mauve paint on their golf club-heads does not mean that they are right for you as a female golfer. Properly fit golf clubs know no gender restrictions. They only know that they are matched to exactly how their owner swings.

For more information on this topic, refer to *The Search for the Perfect Golf Club:* "How About a Break?" (pg. 182) and "What Are These Clubs Any-way?" (pg. 180).

Myth 8

I'll just cut down a set for my kid; that's good enough.

Earl Woods, Tiger's father, has probably spawned more fantasies in the minds of young fathers than the last 100 issues of *Playboy Magazine*. Beats there the heart of a father that didn't quicken when he saw Tiger hugging his father after winning his first Masters in 1997? Yet, despite all that, there is one thing that Earl has consistently said that seems to get consistently lost in the hoopla: "I always made sure that Tiger had clubs that fit."

Let me put it this way. If you want to make dead certain that your little Tiger or Annika will develop a swing that has no chance of succeeding, all you have to do is cut down a set of your clubs and give them to them. They will be too heavy, too stiff, the wrong loft, the wrong lie, and probably the wrong length. Other than that, they will be just what the kid needs to develop a great swing ... for cutting firewood.

Should you perhaps cut one down just to find out if he or she will enjoy taking cuts at a golf ball? Sure, that makes sense, although you might first try to hunt for a single junior club these days for $5 to $10 at a used sports equipment store. As soon as you hear them ask for another bucket and complain about leaving the range too soon, that's the time to get them some proper clubs which are fitted to their size, strength, and athletic ability.

Since 2000, there are a couple of companies who have made a real niche for themselves in offering good quality premade junior sets. Lofts are friendly, shafts are more flexible, weights are a little lighter, and grips are smaller. They offer the sets in pre-made categories of "age 5–8" and "age 9–12" with the substantial difference being their lengths, judged on the basis of average heights for kids in these two age groups.

The only drawbacks to the premade junior sets may be their price and the possibility that your junior happens to be outside the "national average" for height for their age from which the standard lengths of these sets are created. Thus, we come back to your local professional clubmaker who can custom build junior a set as well. And don't panic about that "custom built" part. It's been my experience that the vast majority of clubmakers do not charge prices for their junior clubs that come even close to the prices you would pay for the premade premium branded junior sets found in retail golf shops.

You have to resist the temptation to buy clubs that are too long with the expectation that they will "grow into them." They might well do that, but if they are too long, you are forcing them to hit with something that may very likely cause them to develop a bad swing just to handle the longer length; and you know how hard it is to UN-learn that bad swing.

If that means you need to get them a new set every year or two, get over it. As long as your kid is really into the game, it's a better deal than those tap-dancing lessons you sprang for, not to mention the $125 glow-in-the-dark basketball shoes they just had to have (this month anyway). You're giving them a gift that will literally keep giving for the rest of their lives, long after you're gone. That's no small thing. Besides, it's a small price to pay for watching your son walk up the eighteenth fairway at Augusta with a 12-stroke lead, or your daughter take that dive into the pond at the Dinah Shore, right?

For more information on this topic, refer to *The Search for the Perfect Golf Club*: "Clubs for Your Blooming Tiger or Annika" (pg. 209).

Myth 9

My club is just like the one Tiger uses.

Not...on...your...life.

The clubs you buy in the retail stores are to the clubs the pros use as the Chevy Monte Carlo in your driveway is to the car Jeff Gordon drives in NAS-CAR races. Let me use a set of Payne Stewart's clubs as an example.

In 1999, I had the pleasure of designing what tragically turned out to be the last set of clubs Payne Stewart played in competition. His set required four separate visits to my workshop over the course of six months.

Payne had just concluded a contract with Spalding that required him to play the company's investment-cast cavity-back irons, but he was most anxious to get back to playing with a forged carbon-steel design. I kept spare "raw forgings" from a Lynx set that I had earlier designed for Spalding for just such projects as Payne's.

Payne's first visit was to find out what he liked to see in the various irons as he set up behind the ball. In other words, what kind of leading-edge shape, topline thickness and shape, toe shape, top-of-the-toe transition to the topline, the offset, how the bottom of the hosel should fan out into the blade (indelicately called the "crotch"), and many other subtle areas of each ironhead. Between visits one and two I ground, filed, bent, and formed each of Payne's preferences into each head in the set.

During his second visit, Payne stood right next to me as I reground and shaped each head to a nearly final form. Payne would insert a shaft in each head, assume an address position, look, look again, scratch his head, and, in whatever way he could, express what was good, bad, or indifferent about each one. From this, I now had a much clearer picture of what he wanted and could final grind each head after he left. Matters like center of gravity positions were my responsibility to manipulate in accordance with the ball flight trajectory wishes that Payne had expressed.

During the third and fourth visits, the still not completely finished heads were assembled with different shaft options. Payne hit shot after shot with each club, commenting only when he felt it appropriate to clarify his desires for the feel of both the clubhead and the shaft during the shots. Only when Payne gave final approval to each club was his job complete, and mine shifted into another gear.

All tour players require a minimum of two identical sets of clubs, one to travel with and one to keep in a safe place, packed and ready to ship. Should the nightmare scenario occur of their clubs being lost or even stolen, they can obtain a duplicate of their old set literally overnight. Because of that requirement, I also had to make templates for each head profile along with all sorts of measurements and photographs that would allow me to remake the backup set completely from scratch without having any of the original clubs to guide me.

All totaled, I probably spent somewhere in the area of 300 hours from start to finish on the two identical sets. It's something you should keep in mind the next time you see an ad implying you will be playing clubs that are "just like the ones the pros use." Trust me. You won't.

> For more information on this topic, refer to *The Search for the Perfect Golf Club*: "Getting 'Fitted': The Ultimate Form of Putting It Together" (pg. 173).

Myth 10

Any club that's not a "brand name" is junk.

Whoa, some real re-education is in order here because among those "unknown" brands you just wrote off are some of the world's finest golf clubheads. Let me give you a bit of insight into the golf business; but, first, I'd like to make a couple of crucial distinctions.

If by a "non-brand name" you mean what some people call "clones," then that is something else entirely. Cloning is where an unscrupulous company will make models that copy every detail of a heavily marketed clubhead, right down to coining a name that might even phonetically "sound like" the model name of the original design. Those heads are often in violation of a patent or trademark and most club companies will vigorously prosecute the people who make them—and the people who *buy* them.

There are also clubs that are known as "knockoffs." These are heads that are similar to better known clubs but do not violate any patents. They are not illegal; but they are also usually not very good deals either. Low-quality foundries that are not skilled enough in their production operations to attract business from serious quality-minded golf companies usually make such knockoff heads. Lofts, lies, and head weights are usually far outside the tight production tolerances delivered by the quality foundries. To save money their metal is often a mixture of remelted scrap with a bit of new material thrown in. These companies and their customers damage the reputation of all the quality-minded component manufacturers because most golfers lump every one of the component companies together into one barrel of bad apples.

But there is also a third category of companies that you would do well to take very seriously.

You are certainly aware of the major golf club companies—you routinely see their names on the pages of the golf magazines or on the caps and visors worn by the pros. What you might not know, however, is that while those companies may *assemble* their clubs, they do not actually *manufacture* anything. Everything they sell—heads, shafts, grips—are made by someone else, somewhere else. Take clubheads for example.

Virtually no golf clubheads are made in the United States anymore. Well over 90 percent of them are made in either Taiwan or Mainland China. That means that the number of foundries that are capable of producing high-quality golf clubheads is finite; there are maybe ten or twelve in the world. *Every* reputable golf club company has their heads made at one (or more) of those foundries. Whether you are talking Callaway, Titleist, or Ping or whether you are talking about my company, Tom Wishon Golf Technology; *the heads come from the same manufacturing foundries*. The same people, using the same materials to the same standards on the same machines, make them.

There are two factors that separate the elite from the common in this business. The first is the quality of design. The finest head designs in the world do *not* necessarily come from brand name, mass-advertised, mass-marketed companies. I will, for example, stack up any Wishon clubhead against any brand name, any day, any time, any where. The difference is that we are not a mass-market company—neither is Rolls-Royce. The reason for that has to do with the next factor.

The second factor is the care and skill with which the club is put together, *custom fit to your specific needs*. That is where the brand names, inherently, cannot compete. My designs, when custom fit, and the clubs of a few companies similar to mine, are not made 100,000 at a time to the same specifications. They are made *one* at a time, to *your* specifications. They are not "one size fits all." They are "one club, one customer, one clubmaker."

You would not confuse a large advertising budget with quality in any other area. Don't do it with golf.

> For more information on this topic, refer to *The Search for the Perfect Golf Club:* "To Clone or Not to Clone" (pg. 65) and "Where Do They Come from, Anyway?" (pg. 66).

Myth 11

I was "custom fitted" at the driving range (or retail store or pro shop).

Maybe you were, and maybe you weren't. There are many definitions of what constitutes "custom-fit golf clubs" or a "custom-fitting session." Let me see if I can describe it this way.

Let's say your car is looking pretty trashed out. At one level, you can hose your car down with water and squirt off the worst of the dirt. That's an improvement. Not great, but better than nothing. At the next level, you can get out the bucket and soap and give the car a good scrubbing. That's even more of an improvement. Or you can pull out all the stops and scrub it, rub it out, wax it, and detail it inside and out. Now you're ready for show time. The point here is that each of the above can be described as "getting the car washed."

Getting custom fitted for golf clubs is much the same. There are several levels, and all can (and have) been used to describe "custom-fit clubs."

Let me give you a quick summary here, but in the appendix to this booklet I have placed a checklist that will help you to determine whether you are getting a real custom fitting or not. Please take a look at that list any time someone tells you they are going to "custom fit" you for golf clubs.

Level One: Hitting some shots with provided clubs at a driving range or retail store. This is a trial-and-error "Demo Day" approach. You can be fitted with any club you want—as long as it's one of theirs and they happen to have it in stock.

Level Two: This is "Demo Day" on vitamins. You hit several drivers while an electronic device called a launch monitor analyzes your swing. Assuming the $9/hour sales person has a clue as to what the launch monitor is telling him, again, you can be fitted with any club you want—as long as it's one of theirs already sitting on a rack. Another Level Two fitting is grabbing a club or three from a nifty "fitting cart" parked on the range. This is fine for measuring one or two fitting parameters, but not the 20 or so factors that a professional clubmaker can individually tailor for your swing.

Level Three: Now we're getting into what I consider to be a true custom fitting. It usually starts with you being interviewed concerning your past playing tendencies and desired improvements. You will then be manually measured for club length and electronically measured for swing speed. From this information, the clubmaker will present you with a variety of shafts, grips and heads that he feels are acceptable. You make your choices from among those recommendations. Next, he will build a pilot club that you can test out, and alterations will be made from there. After this test period, needed changes will be noted and the final club built.

Level Four: This level would consist of everything mentioned in Level Three, plus a detailed analysis of your existing set and a careful analysis of the proposed set as it is being built. Attention is paid to matching shaft frequencies or club MOI, swing weights, loft and lie tweaking, grip buildups, spine aligning, dead weight, balance point and so forth. This process, exclusive of the club building, takes about eight hours or so spread over multiple visits. This is the rubbed-out, waxed, and detailed version of our car wash.

And like the car wash, each of those four levels could be described as being a "custom fitting," but do you see the differences? Without the right information the person is simply guessing—and he's using your wallet to guess with. That's why I recommend true custom fitting, done by a professional clubmaker, so strongly.

> For more information on this topic, refer to *The Search for the Perfect Golf Club:* "Getting 'Fitted': The Ultimate Form of Putting It Together?" (pg. 173).

Myth 12

Custom fit golf clubs are only for really good golfers.

Nope! The truth is exactly the reverse of that.

Look at it this way. The pros and very low handicappers are skilled enough to be able to play well with almost *any* golf club. You, on the other hand are not; which means YOU need properly fitted golf clubs even more than THEY do. *You need custom fit clubs to minimize your swing errors and to maximize your swing strengths.*

Now, let's be clear—I am NOT saying you can "buy" skill as a golfer. I am not saying that by spending enough money, you can somehow go from being a double-digit handicapper to qualifying for next year's U.S. Open. Buying new clubs—even truly custom built ones—is NOT a substitute for learning and "grooving" the proper swing fundamentals. Never has been. Never will be.

I AM saying, however, that equipment that doesn't fit—that is the wrong length, or loft, or weight, or balance—can keep you from being all that you could be as a golfer (at any level), and it might even keep you from becoming a golfer at all, what with the fact that some three million golfers leave the game every year.

The idea of custom fitting is to have clubs in which the individual design characteristics of the clubhead, shaft, and grip are matched to your swing. Further, they are assembled to allow you to maintain essentially the same swing throughout the set, yet give predictably different distance and trajectory results because of the way each club is designed and built.

This is the essence of clubmaking and design. Unfortunately, that almost never happens because so few golfers ever do more in their search for their perfect golf clubs than to drive to the local golf store or click on their computer.

The average golfer could lose five to six strokes by simply realizing that the golf club is not a "club." It is not something that is used to beat things into submission. It really IS a superbly designed, surgical-quality instrument—*if you take the time to discover how it can be fitted to complement your swing.* The idea here is to play the game with one swing and 14 controlled results—NOT 14 swings and 144 prayers.

Yes, it's true, golf is inherently a difficult and often frustrating game; but that's part of its charm, part of the fun. As with any game, however, if poor equipment rigs the game so you can't possibly win, suddenly it becomes a whole lot less charming and not fun at all.

> For more information on this topic, refer to *The Search for the Perfect Golf Club:* "An Introduction You Really Need to Read" (pg. xv) and "When It Really Becomes Magic" (pg. 178).

APPENDIX

A custom fitting checklist

Read and check which of the following statements applied to your fitting experience. Then, go through the list and note the category at which your check marks stop.

ZERO: Don't bother to waste your time or your money

_____ None of the following statements are true.

POOR: Better than nothing, but not by much

_____ I hit some shots at a driving range (or into a net) with provided clubs and that's it.

_____ I was physically measured for club length.

_____ I was measured (or evaluated) for grip size.

GOOD: Probably a competent fitting

_____ I was electronically measured for swing speed.

_____ I was electronically measured on a launch monitor.

_____ I was interviewed concerning my past playing tendencies and desired improvements.

_____ I was offered a selection of heads from more than one brand and from more than what was immediately available on site.

_____ I was offered a selection of shafts from more than one brand and from more than what was immediately available on site.

_____ I was offered a selection of grips from more than one brand and from more than what was immediately available on site.

EXCELLENT: You'd have to be a PGA Tour pro to do much better than this.

_____ I was built a pilot club that I could test.

_____ Attention was paid to the club composition of the set that was being built.

_____ Attention was paid to the length, loft, and lie of the set (or club) that was being built.

_____ Attention was paid to the shaft frequencies (or club MOI) and swing weight of the set (or club) that was being built.

_____ Attention was being paid to grip buildups, spine aligning, dead weight, and balance point of the set (or club) that was being built.

_____ The fitting process was done over multiple visits.